# Contents

# A rich and ancient land

*India and her neighbours are home to one of the oldest and most brilliant civilizations in the world.*

The Indian subcontinent comprises six countries: India, Pakistan, Bangladesh, Nepal, Bhutan and Sri Lanka. Their combined population totals over one billion people. Although some of the political borders defining these countries are quite young – Bangladesh was only formed in 1971 – India and her neighbours are home to one of the oldest and most brilliant civilizations in the world.

Many different regional cultures and languages have flourished in India's past. In the modern state of India today the government recognizes at least a dozen principal languages, plus many minor ones. The subcontinent is also renowned for its religious diversity. India was the birthplace of the religions of Hinduism, Buddhism, Jainism and Sikhism and since the 10th century has also had a large Muslim population.

**At independence in 1947 the old provinces of the Punjab and Bengal were split between the new countries of India and Pakistan. This map shows the country borders as they are today and the province boundaries when Britain ruled India.**

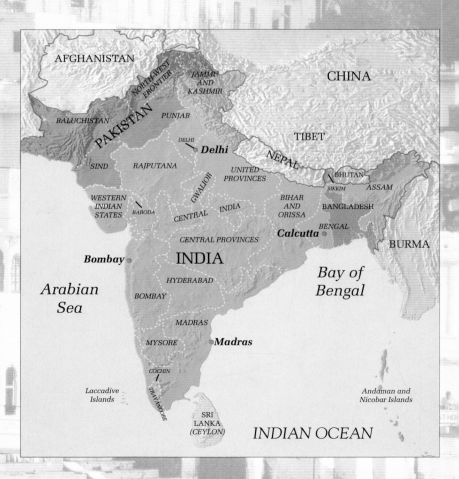

# IMMIGRANTS

# From the Indian Subcontinent

## Katherine Prior

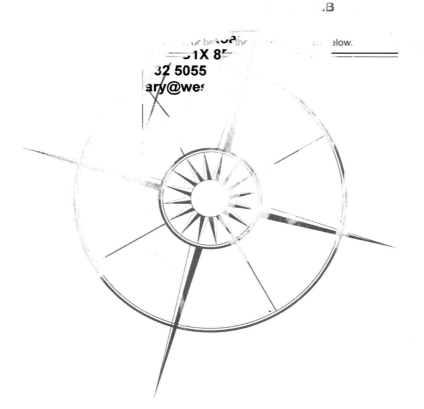

# W
## FRANKLIN WATTS
### LONDON • SYDNEY

*Originally published as Origins: Indian Subcontinent*

This edition first published in 2002

© Franklin Watts 1996, 2002

Franklin Watts
96 Leonard Street, London EC2A 4XD

Franklin Watts Australia
56 O'Riordan Street
Alexandria, NSW 2015

Series Editor: Rachel Cooke
Designer: Simon Borrough
Picture Research: Brooks Krikler Research

A CIP catalogue record for this book is available from the British Library

ISBN 0 7496 4535 0 (pbk)

Dewey Decimal Classification 954

Printed in Malaysia

**Picture acknowledgements**

*t=top; b=bottom; m=middle; r=right; l=left*
Hulton Getty Collection pp. 3, 8t, 9b, 11b, 14t, 24t
James Davis Travel Photography pp. 4, 10b, 25t
The British Library OIOC pp. 5t, 7t, 21t, 23
Ancient Art and Architecture Collection p.5m
Trip Picture Library pp. 5b, 7b, 15 (both), 17b, 18b, 20t, 22t, 29b
Mary Evans Picture Library pp. 6t, 8b, 10t, 19t
Eye Ubiquitous pp. 6 (m and b), 7 (both), 25b, 26b, 27t, 28t
The Hutchison Library pp. 9t, 11t, 20b, 27b, 28b
The Foreign and Commonwealth Office Library Collection p.12
The Mansell Collection p.13 (both)
Tom Donovan Military Pictures p.14b
Life File pp. 17t, 29t
Paul Nightingale pp. 18t, 26t
United States Department of Agriculture p.19b
Frank Spooner Pictures pp. 21b, 22b, 24b
Map by Julian Baker

**The Europeans arrive**

India was celebrated throughout Europe and Asia for the richness of its agricultural lands and its handicrafts which it traded all around the world. The wealth of India soon lured European traders to its shores. From the late 15th century onwards, Portuguese, Dutch, French and British trading companies all attempted to establish a foothold in India in order to buy up spices, such as pepper and cinnamon, and textiles to sell in Europe.

Gradually, the British moved ahead of their rivals. In 1765, they gained control of the wealthy eastern provinces of Bengal, Bihar and Orissa. Their wealth and military strength increased and by 1857 Britain controlled nearly all of the territory which now makes up India, Pakistan and Bangladesh.

▲ Traditionally, most Indians lived in self-sufficient villages.

This wealthy ▶ Mughal prince is wearing fine hand-painted muslin and strings of pearls.

▼ The British introduced trains and the electric telegraph to India.

**The British Empire**

For centuries Indian traders had been calling at ports in South-East Asia and along Africa's eastern coast, but few Indians ever left their country permanently. Under British rule, this changed. Indians were swept into a worldwide empire with colonies in the West Indies, North America, Africa, South-East Asia and Australasia. These colonies produced raw materials, such as sugar, wool, cotton, rubber and tea, for export to British factories and European consumers. Whenever the colonies needed more workers the British encouraged Indians to emigrate as labourers to them.

The British introduced English-language, Western-style education into India. Only a small number of middle-class Indians gained from this, but they discovered that it opened up the rest of the English-speaking world, including the United States of America, to them.

5

## 1947: independence and partition

Indians frequently rose up in rebellion against British rule and by 1920 there was a strong movement for independence. Its principal leader was Mohandas Karamchand (Mahatma) Gandhi, who rallied millions of India's poor peasants in peaceful demonstrations against British rule.

Gandhi championed religious unity between Hindus and Muslims, but his followers were mostly Hindus. Muslims numbered about a third of India's population and feared Hindu domination. In 1947 therefore, when India gained independence, the Muslims chose to have their own country. The Muslim-majority provinces in the west and the east were carved off from India to form West and East Pakistan. Later, in 1971, East Pakistan broke away to form the independent state of Bangladesh.

At independence in 1947, the province of Punjab in the west was partitioned, or divided, between India and West Pakistan and the eastern province of Bengal split between India and East Pakistan. Thousands of Punjabis and Bengalis lost their homes in the upheaval of partition and many of these displaced people chose to emigrate to Britain.

▲ (top) Mahatma Gandhi leads a protest against the British tax on salt.

India contains people of many races, from the Assamese in the lush north-east ▲ to the Rajasthanis in the dry west ▼.

## Indians, Pakistanis and Bangladeshis

In this book, we need to remember the changes in political boundaries that have taken place in the Indian subcontinent in the past 50 years. Up until 1947 most people from British India were referred to as Indians. After 1947, people living in the new country of East and West Pakistan became known as Pakistanis. After 1971, the people of the new country of Bangladesh became known as Bangladeshis, rather than Pakistanis. Indians, Pakistanis and Bangladeshis together are often referred to as South Asians.

# Slavery and indentured labour

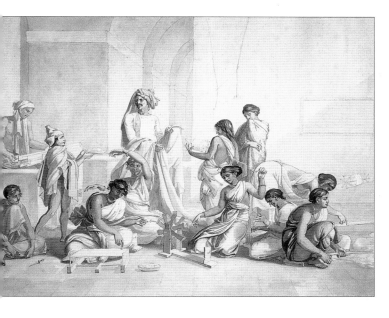

During the 17th and 18th centuries Britain and her European neighbours made vast sums of money growing crops in countries overseas that they had conquered and claimed as their own – their colonies. In North and South America and the West Indies, British, French, Dutch, Spanish and Portuguese colonists grew sugar, tobacco, coffee and cotton. But these crops were labour-intensive – in order to produce them the colonists imported hundreds of thousands of people from Africa and forced them to work on their plantations as slaves.

▲ Indian craft workers were much sought after. These textile workers from South India were taken to the island of Malta by a Frenchman in the late 18th century.

▼ Cane-cutting is exhausting and dangerous work. Tired cane cutters can easily slip and cut themselves with their machete.

## Slaves from India

Most of the slaves were African, but a few came from India. In the 18th century, French colonists on the islands of Mauritius and Bourbon in the Indian Ocean imported over 20,000 slaves from east and south India to work on their sugar plantations.

How did an Indian become a slave? Sometimes, during famines, people sold themselves into slavery simply to avoid starvation. Others, however, were tricked: fit young men were lured on board a slave-trader's ship with the promise of work as sailors and skilled craftsmen were entrapped by the offer of regular employment in Mauritius. Children were kidnapped by local gangs working for French slave-traders. This was the fate that befell Mirham, a 14-year-old Bengali girl, who was snatched from her parents' house near Calcutta in 1785.

Many of the slaves did not live to see Mauritius; almost a quarter of them died from smallpox or other diseases during the voyage there. Most of the survivors were put to work on the sugar plantations, alongside slaves from Africa. Others, however, were employed as cooks, dress-makers, gardeners, stable-boys, carpenters and ordinary labourers.

In the 19th century, Port Louis in Mauritius had a mixed population of African and Indians, often freed slaves, and English and French people.

Tea grown in British colonies was marketed as being produced by 'happy natives', glossing over the hard work of the indentured labourers.

## Life on Mauritius

Once in Mauritius the slaves lost much of their identity as Indians. Many were baptised as Catholics and their owners gave them French names. People named Ramesh or Fatimah became Jean-Paul or Isabelle. Some of the slaves were given cruel or nonsense names, like *Gros Nez* (Big Nose) or *Bon à Rien* (Good for Nothing).

For some of the slaves life in Mauritius, however hard, may have been better than the poverty they left behind in India. But many suffered a dreadful homesickness. Slave-owners and their managers were often cruel, flogging their slaves or reducing their food rations for not working hard enough. Many died of simple illnesses through overwork and lack of medical care. Some slaves were freed and some of the female slaves even married their owners. Most, however, remained enslaved until their death.

## Indentured labourers – the new slaves

In 1834, after years of protest by anti-slavery campaigners, the British government ruled that all slaves within British territories had to be freed. The plantation-owners in the tropical colonies needed another source of cheap labour.

Mauritius had been captured by the British from the French in 1810 so slavery became illegal there, too. Because the planters already had experience of Indians as workers, they decided to try importing Indian labourers, known as coolies, to replace the freed slaves. The labourers were indentured: this means they were contracted to work for a fixed wage for a set period of time, usually five years. In addition to their pay, the planter was obliged to give them basic accommodation, food rations and medical care.

An Indian woman picking tea. She carries the harvested leaves in the sacks slung across her shoulders.

In the 19th century, many Indian peasants like these agreed to become indentured labourers in the hope of escaping the poverty that was often part of their lives.

Anti-slavery campaigners argued that indentured labour was simply slavery under a new name. In spite of their opposition, however, the despatch of Indian labourers to British colonies continued for over 80 years, until 1917. Indians were also sent to Dutch Guiana (Surinam) and the French colony of Reunion, near Mauritius. The British colonies which received most Indians were Mauritius (almost 500,000), British Guiana or Guyana (240,000), Trinidad (144,000), Natal in South Africa (150,000) and Fiji (61,000). Indian labourers also went to Malaya (Malaysia) and Singapore. About two-thirds of the labourers stayed on after the expiry of their contracts and today in Fiji, Guyana and Mauritius, Indians make up half or more of the total population.

## Who were the labourers?

Most of the indentured labourers were Hindi-speaking peasants, usually Hindus, from the north Indian plains. They were recruited by private recruiting agents who received a commission for every labourer they engaged.

The agents often exaggerated the attractions of indentured labour. Most Indians who signed up did so because they were poor or destitute. During famines the recruiting agents had plenty of volunteers, but when the harvests were good, work was plentiful so the recruiters tried to trick people into becoming labourers, sometimes by pretending to be working for the government. Women, especially young widows, who had a low social status, were often kidnapped by recruiters.

**A British-owned tea plantation in Ceylon (Sri Lanka) where labourers imported from India do the hard work. British men have the easy job of supervising them.**

## On the plantations

On arrival the labourers were assigned to their new bosses and put to work. In most of the colonies this meant work on sugar plantations, but in Natal Indians also worked on cotton plantations and the railways and in coal-mines. Many were shocked to discover how hard they were expected to work. A few labourers were blessed with a kind master, but all were treated as prisoners on their estates. They were not allowed to leave without their boss's permission and for running away, being late, working slowly or faking illness they were flogged, put into stocks or imprisoned. Their pay was docked for small faults.

Away from India it was difficult for the labourers to keep up their culture. Whereas in India, many would have chosen a husband or a wife according to strict rules laid down by their community, in Mauritius, the West Indies, Natal or Fiji, these rules were broken. Hindu and Muslim customs were hard to preserve and the type of religion the labourers practised became much simpler. Not knowing anything of the cultural traditions the labourers had left behind, the Europeans in the colonies looked down upon them as 'dirty coolies' – ignorant and uncivilized.

**Indentured labourers had to struggle to maintain their religion and culture abroad but many held on to their beliefs. This mosque is in Port of Spain, Trinidad.**

◀ **Indian traders often followed the indentured labourers to the colonies. This cheerful Indian snack-seller is from Penang in Malaysia.**

▼ **Mahatma Gandhi studied law in Britain. He used the knowledge he gained to fight for the rights of Indian labourers in South Africa.**

## Staying on

Initially many labourers returned home at the end of their period of indenture but after the 1850s most opted to stay on in their new country, usually because they had better economic prospects there than back in India. In Trinidad and Fiji, for example, the labourers were encouraged to swap their return passage for a grant or cheap lease of farming land. Even as free labourers, however, the Indians had few opportunities for education. Most remained in the countryside as market gardeners, small farmers and petty shopkeepers.

By the end of the 19th century, influential Britons and Indians were calling for an end to indentured labour, but it was Mahatma Gandhi, India's great nationalist leader, who did most to end the system. For 20 years, from 1894 until 1914, he fought for political and civil rights for Indian labourers in Natal in South Africa. He rallied such opposition to the system, both in India and Britain, that the British were forced to phase it out. Indentured labour virtually ceased after 1917.

## Free emigration to East Africa

Between 1896 and 1902 almost 40,000 Muslims and Sikhs from the Punjab were indentured by the British to construct the Kenya-Uganda railway in East Africa. Although nearly all of them returned home, they left behind them enterprising traders from Gujarat who had come to East Africa to sell them basic necessities while they built the railway. Gradually these traders set up small shops throughout East Africa, selling cheap manufactured goods. Some established sugar plantations and cotton-processing factories. More Indians arrived to take up jobs in the British colonial administration of East Africa. They staffed the post-offices, the police-stations and the army. By 1948 Kenya had 87,000 Indian residents, Uganda had 35,000 and Tanganyika (Tanzania) had 46,000.

**Indentured labourers from the Punjab working on the Kenya-Uganda railway. When completed the railway opened up the whole of East Africa to European trade.**

# Introductions to Britain

*Indian troops fought on behalf of the British in both World Wars.*

In the two hundred years that Britain ruled India, thousands of Indians came to Britain. Some, such as princes or cricket-players, were wealthy or famous. Most, however, were ordinary people – servants, sailors, students and soldiers.

## Nannies

In the early 18th century, British administrators and soldiers returning from India began to bring back with them Indian domestic servants, often nannies or ayahs. Some hired a nanny just to look after their children during the voyage home and, upon arrival, terminated her employment. Women like this were stranded until they could get a similar job on an outgoing voyage to India. With little or no money, some took to begging in the streets. In the late 19th century an Ayahs' Home was opened in Hackney in east London, which gave the nannies shelter and helped them find work.

## Sailors

During the 18th and 19th centuries much of Britain's commercial shipping was manned by lascars – sailors, often Muslims, from East Bengal, the Punjab and the west coast of India. At only one-sixth the cost of a European sailor, the lascars were cheap to hire. Along with Chinese and African sailors, they were often to be seen around the docks of east London, Southampton and Liverpool. Some were simply waiting for new engagements; others had deserted their ships because they had been maltreated, underpaid or underfed. Their numbers fluctuated, but during the 19th century there were often 2000 or more lascars temporarily resident in London. Muslim lascars continued to work on British ships and, after independence in 1947, they were some of the first people from East and West Pakistan to settle permanently in Britain.

▲ An Indian ayah with the young British child she was hired to look after.

▼ An Indian pedlar, perhaps a deserter sailor, tempts a British housewife with exotic cloth.

The wealthy Indian boys who were sent to English public schools often proved to be brilliant cricketers. Cricket tours between England and India began in the 1880s.

## Students

From about the 1850s, wealthy Indian families began enrolling their sons at English public schools and universities. Two of India's most famous nationalist leaders, Mahatma Gandhi and Jawaharlal Nehru, as well as the founding father of Pakistan, Muhammad Ali Jinnah, were educated in England. These young men and many like them returned to India brimming with ideas about parliamentary democracy, free speech and racial equality.

## Soldiers

The British maintained a large army in India and frequently used it outside of India. Its officers were British, but most of its soldiers were Indian, often Sikhs from the Punjab. Indian troops fought overseas on behalf of the British in both World Wars. Many thousands died.

For a lot of the soldiers, being sent overseas was an eye-opener. Some were surprised to discover that Europe had poor people. Others marvelled that so many women could read; they were used to only men knowing how to read. In each case the survivors' stories made their families and neighbours think about the possibilities of going abroad, especially to Britain. After the Second World War, former Sikh soldiers were among the first Indians to emigrate to Britain.

Indian soldiers fought on behalf of the British in both World Wars. Many were decorated for bravery.

# Post-War immigration to Britain

*'We are lucky that we have our relatives here ... sometimes I feel as though I live in my village.'*

Up until 1945 only a few thousand Indians had settled in Britain permanently, but after the Second World War there was a huge shortage of labour in Britain. Thousands of West Indians, Indians and Pakistanis came to Britain to take up low-paid manual jobs in factories and construction. Indian and Pakistani immigration peaked in the 1960s and by 1971 there were about 750,000 South Asians living in Britain, nearly all of them in England.

▼ Establishing places of worship was important for the first immigrants. These Sikhs are singing hymns at a gurudwara in Southall, London.

► Indian and Pakistani immigrants to Britain, like this Sikh toy-seller in London, were soon opening up shops to serve their communities.

## The first immigrants

Some of the first Indian workers to come to Britain after the war were Sikh peasants and former soldiers from the Punjab. Many of them had lost their farming land in 1947 when the Punjab had been split in two between the new countries of Pakistan and India.

Initially many Sikhs came as single men, leaving their wives and children behind in India or Pakistan, but gradually they began to bring their families over to join them and by the early 1960s there were distinct Sikh communities in London and the Midlands. The first gurudwara, or Sikh temple, opened in Southall in south-west London in 1962.

▲ For many years the Muslim community in Britain consisted only of men, as the workers left their wives and children behind in Pakistan or Bangladesh.

▼ As immigrant communities grew in Britain, advertising appeared in South Asian languages. This British poster written in Bengali is advertising rice.

Another group of post-War immigrants were Muslim men from West Pakistan and East Pakistan (now Bangladesh). Like the post-War Sikh immigrants, they came from rural areas and lacked skills for urban life. They too took on a lot of dirty, poorly-paid jobs, that no-one else wanted. Initially, they settled in east London but, as their numbers increased, they found work further afield in the textile and heavy engineering factories around Manchester, Birmingham and Bradford. In some factories in these cities in the 1960s and 70s, over 95 per cent of the night-shift workers were Pakistanis.

## A temporary move?

These men did not expect to settle in Britain and so for many years they left their wives and daughters in Pakistan. By the early 1970s, however, most had accepted that their migration was permanent and they began to bring their womenfolk to Britain. Until then, the young Muslim men did not have a regular family life and lived in crowded dormitories where the night-shift and day-shift workers took it in turns to sleep. By living cheaply in Britain they could afford to save money to invest in land and good housing back in their home country.

Hindus from the western Indian state of Gujarat also came to Britain. Many of these settled in the Midlands, especially around Leicester.

কম দামে ভাল চাউল টিলডা পাটনা চাউল

## Discrimination at work

In 1962 the British government began to restrict free immigration to Britain. From 1967 onwards the only West Indians, Indians and Pakistanis to be allowed into Britain were those with close family relations already settled there. Immigrants were accused of taking away jobs from British-born workers and pushing down wages. These fears were frequently exaggerated; nevertheless they helped to foster an atmosphere of resentment against the immigrants.

British employers were slow to accept that the South Asians could do skilled jobs; it was not until 1970 that an Indian was accepted into the police force. The immigrants also faced hostility from English workers and trade unions. Many labour organizations insisted that all workers should be treated the same and refused to make allowances for the immigrants' different religious beliefs and cultural practices, such as wearing turbans with uniforms.

▲ Today, Sikh men can join the British police without having to give up their turban which is part of their religious identity.

▼ The first generation of South Asian women in Britian often worked in all-women factories like this seamstress.

## Working women

Many of the Sikh and Hindu women went out to work, often doing low-paid assembly-line work in factories. Most Muslim women did not go out to work because their husbands and fathers did not want them coming into contact with men from outside the family. Instead, they worked from home, doing long hours of piece-work sewing. In the 1970s for each garment they made they earned a tiny sum, perhaps as little as 10 pence per dress.

# Immigrant communities

Most of the first generation of immigrants from the Indian subcontinent socialized within their own communities. A Muslim man who settled near Manchester in the 1960s says: 'We are lucky that we have our relatives here, we live nearby, we help each other when the need arises, we do not feel lonely – sometimes I feel as though I live in my village.'

Immigrants' social lives revolved around their places of religious worship. Gurudwaras for Sikhs, mosques for Muslims and Krishna and Rama temples for Hindus all acted as meeting places and employment agencies, as well as places of worship.

▲ As the immigrants settled into Britain, they began importing their favourite foods like green chillies and white radishes.

# Helping one another

At first the immigrants had difficulties getting access to regular banking facilities and mortgages, so they often clubbed together and lent one another money. Gujaratis in particular have a history of being successful traders and bankers, and it was not long before they were helping one another to begin small ventures, such as corner-shops, restaurants, newsagents and mini-cab companies.

Nowadays, many second-generation immigrants are qualifying as doctors, accountants, engineers and lawyers and are making their way in modern Britain. But this has often been achieved by their parents' willingness to work long hours in a country where they have been isolated from most of the population.

▼ Immigrants placed a high-value on education for their children. Many of the second generation have become highly qualified professionals, such as this doctor.

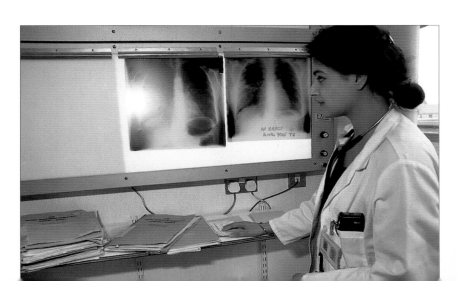

# To America and Australia

Indians first began emigrating to North America in the 1890s and 1900s. The first immigrants were Sikh labourers from rural Punjab. Some found work on the railways and in lumber camps in British Columbia in Canada. Others found work in the United States on farms and orchards in California and in saw-mills in Oregon and Washington. The first immigrants were nearly always young men who travelled with a male relative or friend from their village. They did not intend to settle in North America; they simply wanted to earn money for their families to invest in farming land in the Punjab.

## A hostile reception

There were never more than a few thousand Punjabi immigrants in either Canada or the USA, but by about 1907 racist groups, such as the Asiatic Exclusion League, began to panic. Newspapers complained of the 'Tide of Turbans' and the 'Hindu invasion' and carried hostile stories about Indian religious customs with headlines like 'Hindus Cover Dead Bodies with Butter'.

**In the 1890s and 1900s work in the lumber industry attracted Indians to western Canada. Local lumberjacks often resented the competition from the Indian workers.**

**Early Indian immigrants to the United States were often employed as fruit pickers in the orange orchards of California.**

▲ Many of the first Indian immigrants to Canada were Sikhs. Today the Sikh community there is a strong one.

▼ Indians also found jobs in food processing and canning factories in California.

Workers' organizations also campaigned for restrictions on Indian immigration because they feared that their readiness to work for low wages would force wages down. In September 1907, local lumberjacks in Bellingham, Washington, herded together over 200 Indian immigrant labourers and drove them out of the town, savagely beating some of them and inflicting serious injuries.

Fears about an 'Asian invasion' prompted action from the governments of both the United States and Canada. Indian immigration was effectively stopped to Canada from 1908 and to the United States from about 1911. Indians did not give in meekly to these laws. Several Indians took the United States government to court to challenge decisions denying them American citizenship. But the laws caused the existing communities to shrink. Numbers of Indians in North America dwindled from the 1920s until after the Second World War.

## Australia

A similar situation developed in Australia, where throughout the 19th century a trickle of labourers came from India as shepherds and sugar-cane workers, pedlars and camel-train drivers. By the end of the 19th century small pockets of Muslims and Sikhs from the Punjab had established themselves as banana-growers in northern New South Wales and Queensland. Labour organizations, however, were hostile to the importation of coloured labour. In 1901 their opposition plus the racial prejudice of white settlers prompted the new Australian government to ban non-European immigration to Australia. This immigration policy was known as the White Australia Policy; it was not fully repealed until 1973.

## Immigration by qualifications, not race

Immigration laws in the United States, Canada and Australia began to change after the war. In 1946 the United States agreed to admit a maximum of 100 immigrants from India per year and ruled that Indians were now eligible for American citizenship. Then, in 1965, the government abolished race as a basis for immigration policy and declared instead that America would take people from any country if they had professional skills that America needed. In 1967 Canada made a similar ruling. Australia did not immediately abandon the use of racial categories in immigration policy, but from 1966 people of any race who had useful professional qualifications were invited to apply for entry.

From the 1960s onwards, the Indian presence in the United States, Canada and Australia changed from a shrinking number of labourers and farmers to a growing city-based, professional population. Doctors, engineers, scientists and academics were

▲ Before the railways were built, camel-drivers from north-west India carted goods across Australia's vast deserts.

▼ This professor of robotics is one of the many highly qualified Indians working in the United States.

▲ **Born in Australia, this boy is attending an Islamic centre in Brisbane to learn about his religion and culture.**

▼ **This South Asian woman in New York still wears her traditional *salwar kameez*, a type of pyjama suit.**

the new Indian immigrants. They arrived in considerable numbers. From 1960 until 1975 about 100,000 people born in India emigrated to the United States. By 1987 there were an estimated 500,000 South Asians in the country. Many were Gujaratis and Maharashtrians from the city of Bombay in western India or Tamils from the city of Madras on India's south-east coast. Australia and Canada's South Asian population began to grow steadily too, with almost 230,000 settling in Canada by 1987 and 100,000 in Australia.

As educated professionals, fluent in written and spoken English, the newcomers from India and Pakistan usually found skilled employment quickly. They did not suffer the amount of abuse and racial prejudice meted out to the labourers who had emigrated in the 1900s and 1910s. They earned good incomes and were able to buy homes for themselves in comfortable middle-class suburbs.

## A sense of not belonging

Nevertheless, settling into North America or Australia was not always easy for these people. Many found their new life isolating and unfriendly. As one Indian woman in the United States explained: 'We stand out. We wear saris. We look different. I experience a sense of "I don't belong here". I don't feel involved here. Sometimes I feel homesick.'

To combat the sense of not belonging, the immigrants tended to stick together, marrying within their own communities and preserving a traditional way of life in their homes. Indeed many of the first generation of post-war immigrants adopted two styles of life – a Westernized one for their working day and an Indian or Pakistani one for their home life.

# Refugees and outcasts

*The descendants of the early Indian emigrants discovered that the original inhabitants still looked upon them as foreigners.*

During the 19th century, as we have seen, the British authorities in India organized and encouraged the emigration of Indians to other British colonies. Gradually, as these colonies attained their independence from the British, the descendants of the early Indian emigrants discovered that the original inhabitants still looked upon them as foreigners. Even though they had been born in the colony and might never have been to India, the local population resented their presence.

**When Britain ruled both India and Burma, many Indian mahouts (elephant drivers) worked in Burma in the teak wood industry.**

## Burma

Burma, one of India's largest neighbours, was a British colony until 1948 and many Indians had gone there to work. After independence, the Burmese government continued for a time to tolerate the presence of half a million Indians in the country. The Indian population filled many labouring jobs, but also included influential bankers, traders and manufacturers. In 1962, however, the new government of General Ne Win ordered all Indians to depart. By 1964 over 300,000 Indians had returned to India, stripped of all their property and wealth. The few who remained disguised their Indian origins, adopting Burmese names and styles of dress.

## East Africa

In the early 1960s the Indians resident in the colonies of East Africa – Kenya, Tanzania and Uganda – regarded the approaching end of British colonialism with uncertainty. Many knew their strength in commerce and manufacturing was resented by the black African population. As each colony gained independence, it introduced policies designed to oust Indians and Europeans from trade, industry and government service. Thousands of East African Indians emigrated to Britain. By 1981, 155,000 Indians of East African origin were living in Britain.

## Leaving Uganda

The Indian exodus was most dramatic in Uganda, which had gained its independence in 1962. In August 1972, a new president of Uganda, General Idi Amin, announced that all Asians holding British passports would have to leave Uganda within 90 days. Many Indians who had become Ugandan citizens were also forced out. Indian businesses were all compulsorily acquired by the government to be sold to African Ugandans. Indians were allowed to take with them £50 per family and 485 lbs of personal belongings; everything else had to be abandoned. By 1973, most had fled, nearly all of them to Britain.

▼ The Indians who fled Uganda in 1972 arrived at Stansted Airport to a cold and wet Britain. They brought with them only the few possessions they could carry on board the aeroplane, leaving everything else they owned behind in Uganda.

◄ In an Africanization drive, the President of Uganda, Idi Amin, ordered all Asians to leave Uganda.

24

## Fiji

Between 1879 and 1916, over 60,000 Indian indentured labourers were sent to the island of Fiji, mostly from the Hindi-speaking region of north India. In addition a number of Gujarati and Punjabi traders came to Fiji as free immigrants, to cater for the needs of Indian population. By the 1940s, Indians outnumbered the indigenous (or native) Fijians. Many of the labourers had stayed on in Fiji as small farmers and cane growers, but they were not allowed to own any land. Instead, they invested in education and commerce, until Indians controlled most of Fiji's shops and industry and dominated the legal and medical professions.

Fiji's population includes descendants of the Indian labourers, like the policeman on the left, and indigenous Fijians, like the one on the right.

## An anti-Indian coup

In 1970 Fiji gained independence from Britain. Although the new constitution safeguarded the rights of the native Fijian population, the Fijians resented the Indians' command of the island's commercial life. In May 1987 the Fiji army overthrew a newly-elected government, which was backed by the Indian population. The leader of the coup, Lt. Col. Sitiveni Rabuka, explained that he had acted in order to protect the Fijian way of life from the encroachments of the Indians. After the coup many of Fiji's Indian politicians and intellectuals, some of whom had been imprisoned or beaten by the army, fled to Australia and New Zealand. The vast majority of Indians, however, have had no choice but to remain in Fiji. Many worry that they will be permanently locked out of political power. In particular, the future is uncertain for the Indian farmers who are still not allowed to purchase land.

After the coup of 1987, many Indo-Fijians applied for visas to emigrate to Australia. Long queues formed in the rush to leave.

# Indians abroad today

*The descendants of 19th-century emigrants are rediscovering India.*

In the past 200 years several million people from the Indian subcontinent have emigrated permanently to other parts of the world. The experience of those who emigrated as members of the British colonial empire, before Indian and Pakistani independence in 1947, differs greatly from that of the later emigrants.

▲ Music cassettes and video tapes have increased South Asian emigrants' awareness of their shared culture.

Religious leaders, ▶ like this Hindu priest in Malaysia, teach children born out of the subcontinent about their religious traditions.

## Rediscovering India

The emigrants of the colonial period, especially the indentured labourers, retained few links with India. Their religion and culture were diluted and many of their descendants could not fluently speak an Indian language. India became a foreign place to them.

In recent years, however, the government of India has attempted to rebuild links with the descendants of its 19th-century labourers. Students of Indian origin are awarded scholarships to study Hindi in India, while Indian dancers, musicians and writers are sent to Mauritius, Fiji, Trinidad and other former colonies. Religion, too, is increasing the ties with India, as community leaders sponsor tours by priests to preach to local Indian groups. After decades of being cut-off from India, the descendants of Indian indentured labourers are now proudly exploring the culture of their forefathers.

### Tight-knit communities

The post-1947 emigrants, born in the age of aeroplanes and telephones, have found it much easier to retain links with their families in the subcontinent and to preserve their culture. This is most obvious in Britain where Indians, Pakistanis and Bangladeshis are concentrated in tight-knit communities – there are whole suburbs of South Asian households, shops and places of worship referred to as 'little Indias' or 'little Pakistans'.

The geographical concentration of South Asians in Britain means that in several districts the 'Asian vote' is large enough to influence the outcome of an election. Because of this, issues affecting South Asians – such as racial harassment and religious and language teaching in schools – have become part of mainstream British politics.

**Children of South Asian immigrants born in Britain, North America and Australia are growing up in a society of many different races and cultures.**

▲ These men, first-generation immigrants from India, are enjoying their retirement in Britain after a life of hard work.

### The second generation

In Britain today there are perhaps 1.5 million South Asians, of whom about 40 per cent have been born in Britain. In the United States, Canada and Australia too there is now a large population of second-generation Indians and Pakistanis. These young people know no other country than the one they have been born in, but because of their skin colour they are often still regarded as foreigners. Many experience difficulties in trying to fit in with their white friends at school while also living up to their parents' expectations and ideals. Some, for example, do not want their

parents to choose their wife or husband for them. Their parents, on the other hand, often complain that their children are becoming too Westernized. A Gujarati man in Leicester lamented of his seven year old son, 'He can understand some Gujarati but he does not speak it; it upsets my mother, who only knows Gujarati, that she cannot have a conversation with her own grandson.'

The children of modern South Asian immigrants face a different future to that of their parents, especially in Britain. Many of the factory jobs that the first generation of immigrants filled have disappeared. There is a need instead for high-skilled, professional workers. Britain now has a substantial Indian and Pakistani middle class filling this need, much as in the United States, Australia and Canada, but there are still many poor South Asians. In particular, the Bangladeshis, most of whom arrived in Britain in the early 1980s after the demand for unskilled labour had dried up, suffer high unemployment, poor housing, low wages and substandard levels of education and health care. They are also the victims of vicious racial harassment.

▲ This Punjabi family is enjoying a day out at the seaside at Blackpool in Britain, a traditional treat for British families.

▼ The sons of Bangladeshi immigrants to Britain, these boys live in Tower Hamlets, one of the poorest areas in London. They face an uncertain future.

## Fewer opportunities for emigration

People still emigrate from India, Pakistan and Bangladesh, but since the tightening of Britain's immigration laws in the 1960s and 70s and the economic recession experienced in other Western countries, there are fewer opportunities for people to leave. In particular, the doors of other countries are now firmly shut against the poor, unskilled labourers of the subcontinent, even though for over a century it was this class of people who were the workforce of the British empire.

## South Asian attitudes to emigration

The governments of independent India, Pakistan and Bangladesh have not always welcomed emigration. In the 1960s and 70s the government of India discouraged the emigration of its professionals to the United States. Indian politicians resented losing much-needed doctors and scientists to a country which could afford to train its own.

However, since the early 1970s, the governments of India, Pakistan and Bangladesh have encouraged the temporary emigration of hundreds of thousands of contract workers to the oil-rich states of the Middle East. Most of these workers are Muslims, either from Bangladesh and Pakistan or from Muslim areas of India. Their earnings provide a huge boost to the economies of their home countries. During the 1980s, for example, workers in Kuwait and Iraq alone sent back about US$650 million to their families each year. But the labourers, known as guestworkers, enjoy few rights in their host countries.

In recent years, India, Pakistan and Bangladesh have benefitted not only from remittances from emigrants abroad, but also by the children of emigrants coming to the Indian subcontinent as tourists. People of Indian or Pakistani origin now frequently travel there on holiday, eager to see the sights of which their parents or grandparents have always spoken, to meet distant relatives and to explore the villages or home towns of their ancestors.

▲ Labourers from Pakistan and India often seek work in the Middle East, like these men laying drains in Abu Dhabi.

▼ The beautiful new Swaminarayan temple in London, built largely by members of Britain's Gujarati community, is a building that everyone in Britain can be proud of.

# Timeline

| | |
|---|---|
| **c.1300BC** | *Rig Veda*, Hinduism's holiest hymns, written. |
| **6th cen. BC** | Beginning of Buddhism, founded on the teachings of Gautama Buddha (c. 563-483BC). |
| **1st cen. AD** | St Thomas brings Christianity to South India. |
| **712** | Arabs conquer Sind in western India; this is the first impact of Islam on India. |
| **1498** | Portugal's Vasco da Gama is the first European to sail around Africa to India. |
| **1526-1707** | Mughal Empire at its height: the Mughal emperors are Muslims, originally Mongols, who introduce Persian culture and styles of government to India. |
| **1583** | Akbar, 3rd Mughal emperor, receives English ambassadors sent by Queen Elizabeth I. |
| **1608** | English East India Company establishes a factory at Surat in western India. |
| **1631-53** | Shah Jahan, the 5th Mughal emperor, builds the Taj Mahal at Agra. |
| **1765** | English East India Company receives the right from the Mughals to collect taxes for the eastern provinces of Bengal, Bihar and Orissa – the beginning of British government in India. |
| **1834** | British abolition of slavery; system of indentured labour introduced to replace slaves. |
| **1835** | Britain announces the introduction of English-language, Western-style education to India. |
| **1857-58** | The Indian Rebellion or Mutiny: In May 1857 the Bengal army rose up against British rule and was joined in revolt by large sections of the civilian population in northern India. |
| **1885** | Founding of the Indian National Congress, the political party which led the struggle for Indian independence from British rule. |
| **1896** | Indian labourers arrive in East Africa to build the Uganda railway; they are followed by substantial numbers of free Indian immigrants. |
| **1908-11** | The United States and Canada halt Indian immigration. |
| **1914-18** | World War I: Indian army soldiers fight overseas for the British in Mesopotamia, Turkey and France; at home in India war-time shortages and political repression fuel the campaign for Indian independence. |
| **1913-18** | Ghadr Conspiracy: Indians in North America form a revolutionary movement; they attempt to start a rebellion against British rule in India |
| **1914** | *Komagata Maru* affair: immigration authorities stop a boatload of Punjabis from landing in Vancouver, Canada and, despite violent protest from its passengers, the ship, the *Komagata Maru*, is forced to sail back to India. |
| **1917** | End of indentured labour. |
| **1920-22** | Non-Cooperation Movement: Gandhi, India's most famous nationalist leader, organizes a nationwide movement of peaceful strikes against British rule; the same form of protest is followed in 1930-34 in Gandhi's Civil Disobedience Movement. |
| **1939-45** | World War II: Indian soldiers again fight for the British; Indian politicians demand independence in return for Indian support of the war effort and launch the violent Quit India Movement. |
| **1940** | Pakistan resolution: the Muslim League resolves to fight for the creation of Pakistan, a separate homeland for India's Muslim population. |
| **1947** | Independence from Britain and Partition forms the two separate countries of India and Pakistan; partition is followed by severe rioting as Hindus and Sikhs leave their homes in Pakistan to move to India and Muslims leave India to move to Pakistan. |
| **1948** | Mahatma Gandhi assassinated by Hindu fanatic. |
| **1962** | Indians expelled from Burma. |
| **1962** | Free entry to Britain from the subcontinent limited. |
| **1965-73** | The United States, Canada and Australia stop using race to determine their choice of immigrants. |
| **1971** | After fighting a war against West Pakistan, East Pakistan becomes the independent Bangladesh. |
| **1972** | Idi Amin, president of Uganda, orders Asians to leave the country; most flee to Britain. |
| **c.1978-96** | Khalistan movement: militant Sikhs in the Punjab use terrorist tactics to campaign for a Sikh independent homeland; Sikhs in Britain and Canada offer support to Sikhs in India. |
| **1984** | Assassination of Mrs Indira Gandhi, India's Prime Minister, by Sikh militants. |
| **1987** | Coup in Fiji: the elected government, backed by Fiji's Indian population, overthrown by army. |

# Glossary

**assembly line:** a chain-like system of production in a factory where each worker does one specific thing to a product, like tightening a screw, before moving it along a conveyer belt to the next worker who does another specific thing to it.

**Australasia:** the region covering Australia, New Zealand and the islands of the South Pacific.

**ayah:** an Indian nanny.

**Buddhism:** the world religion founded in northern India by Gautama Buddha in the 6th century BC, now practised most widely in south-east Asia.

**colony:** a country or territory which has been taken over by another country and which does not govern itself anymore.

**coloured labour:** non-white workers; this is an old-fashioned term that was often used by white workers in Britain, North America and Australia in the 19th and early 20th centuries.

**commerce:** the buying and selling of things, usually on a big scale.

**commission:** a fee that a recruiting agent received for signing someone up as an indentured labourer.

**coolies:** a word for Indian labourers; calling someone a 'cooly' was also used as an insult.

**coup:** the sudden overthrow of a government by a small group or force.

**destitute:** without money, housing or employment.

**emigrate:** to leave one's country to settle permanently in another country.

**flogging:** beating a person with a whip.

**gurudwara:** a Sikh temple.

**Hindi:** a language spoken in central northern India; now one of the national languages of India.

**Hinduism:** one of the world's great religions originating in India over 4000 years ago. Hindus believe in the supreme God, who is present in all things, but also worship many other lesser gods and goddesses.

**immigrate:** to arrive in a new country intending to stay permanently.

**indenture:** an agreement; a contract.

**indentured labour:** a system whereby a worker signs a contract agreeing to work for an employer for a fixed number of years at a fixed wage.

**Jainism:** a religion founded in northern India in the 5th and 6th centuries BC. Followers of Jainism believe in the sacredness of all life.

**Krishna:** a Hindu god.

**lascar:** an Indian sailor, often a Muslim man.

**lumber:** timber or logs.

**lumberjack:** a worker in the timber industry.

**Muslim:** a follower of Islam, the world religion founded in AD 622 by the Prophet Muhammad in the Middle East. Muslims believe in one God. Their most holy book is the Koran.

**parliamentary democracy:** a political system in which all the people democratically have a say in electing representatives to a central body which makes the laws and governs the country.

**partition:** the division of something in two, such as the partition of British India into the separate countries of Pakistan and India.

**pedlar:** sometimes spelt peddler, a small trader who travels about from house to house with a range of household goods to sell or 'peddle'.

**piece work:** work in which a worker is paid for the number of items that he/she makes instead of the number of hours worked.

**prejudice:** an opinion against someone or something which has been made without knowing anything about that person or subject.

**Rama:** a Hindu god.

**recruiting agent:** someone who was paid to sign up people as indentured labourers.

**refugee:** someone who is fleeing danger; someone who is forced out of their home territory by war, famine or political violence.

**Sikhism:** the religion founded in the early 16th century in the Punjab of northern India by Guru Nanak. Sikhs believe in one God.

**smallpox:** an infectious disease, now thought to be eradicated, causing fever and a severe rash.

# ✻ Index